Another
Miserable
Love Song

Another Miserable Love Song

Brooke Carter

orca soundings

ORCA BOOK PUBLISHERS

Library and Archives Canada Cataloguing in Publication

Carter, Brooke, 1977–, author
Another miserable love song / Brooke Carter.
(Orca soundings)

Issued in print and electronic formats.
ISBN 978-1-4598-1312-0 (paperback).—ISBN 978-1-4598-1313-7 (pdf).—
ISBN 978-1-4598-1314-4 (epub)

I. Title. II. Series: Orca soundings
PS8605.A77777A66 2016   jc813'.6   c2016-900456-2
                     c2016-900457-0

First published in the United States, 2016
Library of Congress Control Number: 2016931880

Summary: In this high-interest novel for teen readers, Kallie tries to get
over her father's death and help her band at the same time.

MIX
Paper from
responsible sources
FSC® C016245
www.fsc.org

*Orca Book Publishers is dedicated to preserving the environment and has
printed this book on Forest Stewardship Council® certified paper.*

Orca Book Publishers gratefully acknowledges the support for its
publishing programs provided by the following agencies: the Government
of Canada through the Canada Book Fund and the Canada Council
for the Arts, and the Province of British Columbia through
the BC Arts Council and the Book Publishing Tax Credit.

Cover image by Getty Images

ORCA BOOK PUBLISHERS
www.orcabook.com

Printed and bound in Canada.

19 18 17 16 • 4 3 2 1

For Robert, and for my girls.
Stay loud.

Chapter One

One good thing about watching a matinee alone on a Thursday afternoon is there's no one around to see you bawl your eyes out. *The Outsiders* always got me—especially the part where Patrick Swayze's character lets down his guard and shows some love for Ponyboy—but this time I was a mess. Maybe it was because it was my eighteenth birthday (which should have been a bonus, seeing as I waited an eternity to say goodbye to seventeen). Or maybe it was because my dad had promised to be there and wasn't. Death has a funny way of preventing you from keeping your promises. Dad used to say, *Kallie, not even death could keep me from our Swayze-fest.* I guess that's another thing death does. It makes liars of us all.

The Outsiders being my all-time favorite book-slash-movie, every year on my birthday my dad and I would visit the run-down Dolphin Cinema on Hastings Street for the dollar-matinee showing. Until this year, when he decided to die.

Scratch that—I shouldn't have said that. Jeremiah Echo would never have chosen to die, and certainly not before we got to see our favorite greaser gang come of age one last time. If he'd known he'd die before seeing Ponyboy bleach his hair or Two-Bit start the day with chocolate cake and beer, well, I'm sure Dad would have arranged a final viewing, no horrible death puns intended. Pancreatic cancer is one swift downer. By the time Dad found out that the dull pain in his side was a super deadly tumor, it was too late. He was gone two weeks later, and I began spending a lot of time in dark movie houses.

Dad had been my best friend. Hanging out with him had been like being with an older, cooler version of myself. It's a little cheesy to say that about your own dad, I know, but Echo Senior was special like that. And seeing as my mom was a deadbeat or maybe not of this earth anymore, and my extended family consisted entirely of distant cousins back in Greece, well, I was on my own.

It was going to be a long walk in the blazing early-July sunlight, and as usual I was ill equipped in the fashion department. I was not meant for a hot climate—not that Vancouver was particularly tropical or anything, but it was muggy as hell in the summer, and I didn't do shorts. Or sundresses. I had some curvy thighs, and I did not want them rubbing together and getting all sweaty or sticking to a janky old bus seat.

I stood in the sunshine and tried to will myself to enjoy the heat, to be one of those gross people who feels energized by the sun instead of cooked by it, but it wasn't happening.

I took out my dad's ancient iPod and started walking. On the playlist? The sad-sad-birthday-after-your-dad-dies-and-you-are-suddenly-homeless playlist? A downbeat mix of Radiohead, Smashing Pumpkins, Nirvana (because my dad loved them the most), Portishead and a little Chopin thrown in for the died-way-too-young factor.

I walked down the side street at a good clip, wanting to get to the main road and the bus stop as soon as possible. It wasn't the worst place in the city to be, but it definitely wasn't the best. When I spotted the old blue van trailing me, suddenly I wished I was one of those kids whose parents had bought them a cell phone. If you don't have a cell phone, you might as well be marooned on a desert island or stranded on the moon. When you're a teen girl alone with a suspicious vehicle following you, being stuck on the moon sounds like a really good option.

The van sped up until it was right alongside me. My heart skipped a beat, and I could feel my pulse bubbling in my throat. I did not want to look, because I felt like if I did, I would be making something happen.

"Hey, hot stuff," a voice said, and I was just about to break into a run when the voice said, "Hey, Kallie, like my new ride? Kallie? Didn't you see me waiting for you?"

I stopped and turned, and relief flooded my body like a warm flush. It was Jamie, my friend, and right then absolutely my most favorite person on the planet. She stopped the van.

"Jamie, Jesus!" I said. I walked over to her.

"Well, okay then," she said, leaning her long arm out the window and tipping her imaginary cap at me. "I'll be your lord and savior if you like, little missy."

I rolled my eyes. "What are you doing here? And where did you get this…thing?"

I took a look at the beast Jamie was driving. It was absolutely enormous—calling it a beast was an understatement. It was long, blue, wide, rusted and vibrating with an intense rumble that made it seem like it was going to fall apart at any second, explode or take off into the stratosphere. Maybe all three.

"This, sweet lady," Jamie said with pride, "is your ride home. And my new tour van. So I wouldn't go insulting it too much. Old Blue here has a sensitive disposition. And"—she lowered her voice—"I'm worried it might quit on me if it hears you."

"Dude," I said. "This thing is not Christine, right? It's not going to hunt us down and kill us, is it?"

Jamie smiled—the same amazing, wide smile that had charmed me into being friends with her a few years back. The first time I met Jamie was when she came to my door looking for donations for the junior football team. I knew who she was because I had heard about this girl who went through hell just to get on the football team, and then there she was at my door, looking for cash. She had come to the wrong place. I guess the guys on the team had given her the crappy 'hood to canvass while they took Plum Hill and Tower Heights. Coming to Northside was not a good strategy.

I opened the door and there she was, giving me a world-class smile. It was a true-blue, weak-knee genuine dazzler. It wasn't fake or put on or practiced. It was sincere, the kind of smile you can feel in your chest. The kind that makes you grin back in a stupor. It was a wide smile too, full of teeth, and her eyes were all crinkled up. It felt like that smile was meant just for me. It felt like that smile was saying I was beautiful, that she was happy to see me, that she liked me, really liked me a lot. Jamie's smile was the warmest I had ever felt, and it came on a day when I was not feeling so good about myself. That smile was a surprise for a girl who never got surprised, and I have loved Jamie for that ever since.

And, in true Jamie style, she had shown up again just when I needed her. This time in her big blue boat of a van.

"Hey," I said. "Were you waiting for me the whole time?"

She shrugged. "Nah. I mean, I figured you'd need a ride after your yearly movie, right? Anyway, can't let you walk home alone around here. And I wanted to show off my new wheels."

"Cool. You could have come to the movie too," I said, but as soon as I had, I knew it wasn't really true.

Jamie, to her credit, just nodded. "It's all good," she said. "You going to get in or what?"

I looked at the van. "I don't know. Maybe I should take my chances on the street."

Jamie revved the engine. "Be careful what you wish for, Kallie." She smiled that infectious smile again, and I felt it lift me up inside.

"Thanks," I said and walked around the front of the van. I opened the passenger door, and the weight of it swinging open nearly knocked me over.

"Jesus," I muttered, hopping in and buckling the ancient seat belt.

"That's me," said Jamie. "Your own personal Jesus."

She pressed on the gas and we lurched forward, tires squealing, and sped off.

On the ride back to my neighborhood, Jamie kept quiet and turned on the radio. She tuned it to a classic-rock station, and the sounds of the music my dad loved so much filled the van as we drove. The windows were rolled down, and the wind stirred up my hair and cooled me off. I relaxed into the cracked leather seat and let my hand float on the breeze. Jamie didn't say a word the whole time, and she gave no indication that she saw me crying. That's just something you don't find in a person all that often. That was my Jamie. One of a kind.

Chapter Two

Jamie waited outside in the beast while I ran into my soon-to-be-ex-home to change. I opened the door and found once again, as I had every single day since Dad died, that the house was too quiet. All I had left of him were his old records and a collection of little notes we called "echoes"—and believe me, we relished how clever we were for coming up with that.

I loved our little house. It was only 650 square feet—super tiny—and perfectly square. Dad had painted it this vivid cobalt blue, and it stood out like a gleaming little gem in a sea of tan and brown suburban homes. Our area of Vancouver wasn't the newest, or the best, but it was a safe enough place, and it had its charm. Our landlady, Mrs. Brahni, had been kind enough to let me stay for a couple of months rent free, but at the end of the summer I would either have to come up with enough dough for rent or get out.

While I couldn't bear the thought of losing my home, right now I felt like I couldn't get out and away fast enough. I rushed into the bathroom to freshen up. Walking in the sun had left me feeling a little swampy, and I needed to splash my face with some water. When I reached for a towel, I noticed a slip of paper nestled in the basket of silly soaps my dad kept on the top of the toilet tank. They were shaped like robots and cars and sunglasses and had horrible scents like *leather* and *ocean floor*. I grabbed the paper and unfolded it. On it was printed a single word:

LIVE

I flipped it over and saw two more words:

LIVE LOUD

An echo from Dad? My heart pounded out an aching tune in my chest, and while I was grateful for that tiny piece of him, part of me wished I hadn't found the note. What did he mean?

I pondered it as I ran out to the waiting van and hopped in.

Jamie lived with her bandmates in an old converted convenience store at the edge of town. Most of the houses around there had fallen into disrepair and were either crack houses or were literally crumbling to the ground.

I felt welcome at her place, and Jamie's bandmates were also my friends. The band was pretty good. They called themselves Fractured, and they played a fast mix of punk and straight-head rock. Some of it was a little too pseudo California punk for my taste, but I would never have said that to Jamie. I'd never want to hurt her feelings.

Cindi Broken was the lead singer. She was completely gorgeous and the main object of Jamie's affection. I didn't like the way she treated Jamie sometimes, like Jamie was an annoyance to her.

Elaine Lee, known as LeeLee, played bass. She'd once had a withering crush on me when we were a bit younger and was the wildest and most totally carefree and rebellious person I had ever met.

She was my hero that way. LeeLee did not give one single fuck. One day I hoped to care as little about what people thought of me as LeeLee did about what they thought of her.

Then there was Dolly Dillon. Boy-crazy guitar virtuoso. Dolly looked like a punk Barbie. She was also one of the smartest people I had ever met, and she had a wicked sense of humor. We would play chess together late at night when everyone else was crashed out. I worried about her a little bit. She had a tendency to dumb herself down for whatever boy she liked.

Anjaly "Jelly" Gill filled out Fractured's sound on keyboards. Jelly was a plus-sized super-goth. She was also a very dark and kind of depressive person. Out of all our friends, I felt she'd had it the worst. Her mom was always drunk and screaming at her. Jelly was definitely the Johnny Cade of our gang.

Last was Jamie. Jamie Foster, drummer. She was the band's anchor. She kept everyone in time, which was hard to do sometimes because Dolly was always trying to speed things up. Jamie with the fantastic smile and the patient nature of a saint. Jamie who was the single best thing remaining in my life—a life that was falling apart faster than I could comprehend.

It really hadn't occurred to me that Jamie might have planned a little something for my birthday. Which was pretty stupid, seeing as Jamie is one of the most thoughtful people ever. But when we pulled up, I spotted a few acquaintances milling about with slicked-back hair and rolled-up jeans— '50s greaser getup.

"Hey, Jamie—" I began, but she cut me off as she parked.

"Kallie, it's your birthday," she said. "We are having a party. Deal with it."

"Yeah, but what's with the outfits? Couldn't you have hipped me to that?"

"And spoil the big surprise? Never!" Jamie grinned, popped out of the driver's seat and raced around the beast to open my door for me.

"My lady," she said, bowing dramatically. "Your soiree awaits."

I sighed. "Fine. But I am so *not* having a good time." I pouted in mock protest.

"We'll see," said Jamie with a mischievous grin.

I couldn't help but grin back.

I walked into the store to a chorus of "Happy birthday!" and "Hey, Kallie" and a few whoops and whistles. Someone called out, "Hey, Misery!" and a few people cheered. At the store, only my closest friends called me Kallie. The rest called me Misery Girl, a nickname I'd earned after stage-diving to Fractured's popular song "Misery" at an all-ages show a year ago.

I looked around and saw that someone had put a plaid tablecloth over the old sagging couch in the main room and had gotten several helium balloons with muscle cars printed on them.

"Mustangs and madras, huh?" I said to Jamie.

"That's not all," she said and nodded at a table laden with cheap beer, bottles of Cherry Coke and a lopsided chocolate cake.

"Thank you," I said, and I meant it. I knew how lucky I was to have friends like these.

"Wait," I said, noting Jamie's bland outfit. "Who are you supposed to be?"

She whipped off her shirt so that she was just wearing jeans and a white undershirt, then mussed up her hair.

"I'm Dallas Winston. You know, when he's all sleepy after getting into a fight, and Ponyboy and Johnny come to him for help?" She grinned.

"Nice," I said.

"Yeah," she said. "I know he's supposed to be bare-chested, but, uh, I can't rock that look just now." She swallowed and looked uncomfortable for a moment.

"I can see it," I said and tousled her hair. "You know that's my favorite part. Dally looks the sexiest then."

Jamie smiled shyly at me. "I'll be your Dallas Winston anytime, babe. If you'll be my Cherry," she added lasciviously.

I swatted her. "Watch your mouth, Dallas Winston. I'm too pure for you."

We both laughed and made our way to the table to grab drinks.

"Cheers, Cherry," said Jamie. "Happy birthday."

"Cheers," I said and took a long drink of my Coke.

The party was getting going, and people were dancing and trying to approximate some kind of demented punk-rock sock hop.

"You know what this party needs?" I asked.

"What?" asked Jamie.

"Some real rock. Why isn't Fractured playing?"

Jamie's expression soured.

"What is it?" I asked.

"Nothing," said Jamie. "Don't worry about it now. It's your party, and I want to have fun."

"Okay," I said, but judging from Jamie's expression and reluctance to talk, I assumed it was pretty bad. I hoped everything was okay with the band.

Jamie cleared her throat. "Um, there was a gift we wanted to give you, Kallie, but we can't because Cindi isn't here."

Ah yes, Cindi, always absent and perpetually unreliable. Cindi arrived late to nearly every gig Fractured had.

I suspected she was the source of Jamie's troubled mood.

"Yeah," said LeeLee. "We were going to sing you a song we wrote called 'Stay Gold,' but we can't because Cindi quit the band."

"What?" I almost spit my drink all over LeeLee.

Jelly nodded. "It's basically the worst thing that's ever happened," she said.

"Well, not the worst, Jelly," said Dolly quietly, and Jelly looked at me apologetically. I did just lose my dad, after all.

"Sorry, Kallie," she whispered in her downbeat manner.

"It's okay," I said. And for a second I really felt like it was.

"What happened?" I turned to Jamie.

She shifted uncomfortably, and Dolly spoke for her.

"That bitch ran off with our rent money and jumped ship to tour with

Weedhead. I heard she hooked up with Morgan, the guitarist."

I looked at Jamie. She was positively stricken.

"Oh, Jamie," I began, but she shushed me with a wave of her hand.

Weedhead was Fractured's main rival, even though the two bands could hardly be compared, in my opinion.

"Whatever," Jamie said. "Good riddance." But it was obviously painful for her.

"Yeah," LeeLee said, then hesitated. "Although…we do have this tour coming up, and now we don't have a singer. I really don't want to give up on that."

Jelly nodded. "Me neither," she said.

"What are we supposed to do?" asked Jamie. "Where are we going to find someone who knows all the songs and can fill in on short notice?"

As if on cue, all eyes in the group instantly turned to me. I stared at them, dumb to their intent for a moment, and then realization dawned on me.

"Whoa. No. Oh, no, no, no." As I protested, they all inched toward me like they were going to envelop me in a mass of desperate punk rocker.

"Kallie," said Dolly in her sweetest tone, "think about this. You know it's perfect."

I could tell by her eyes that she was getting excited.

Jamie nodded. "This could work, Kallie."

"But...but I'm not a singer," I explained. "I can't sing."

"That's not true," said Jamie. "I've heard you sing along to our tracks in the car countless times, and you have a great voice. You actually have a prettier voice than Cindi ever did. And don't try to say you don't know the songs, because we all know you do. Hell, you might know them better than we do."

They all nodded, really getting into the idea now.

"Yeah," said LeeLee. "Plus, we love you!"

I laughed at her sweet remark, but I shook my head.

"Even if I can carry a tune, I can't be a lead singer. I don't know how to do that. I'm not…loud enough," I said.

I didn't know what else to say or how to say it. I had often daydreamed about being onstage with the band, imagining how exhilarating it would feel to express myself to so many people at once. But I'd never actually thought I could do it. I was no Courtney Love, Kathleen Hanna, Grace Slick, no idol you could name.

"Well," said Jamie, "the only way to know for sure is to try."

"Great idea," said Dolly. "I'll tune up."

"Wait. What?" I asked as the girls scattered to their various instruments in the main room.

"Jamie," I hissed, getting angry. "What the hell?"

"What?" she asked innocently.

"I can't do this. Not in front of everyone! I don't know what to do."

"Kallie, chill out. Besides, everyone's going home soon anyway. It'll just be us. Here, have some liquid courage." She reached over and cracked a beer and handed it to me.

I wasn't much of a drinker, mainly because it tends to make me sick and also because I kind of had a problem with it when I was younger. But at the moment I felt I needed it. I grabbed the beer from her and took a long gulp. Then another.

"Whoa, easy," said Jamie.

Defiantly, I tilted my head back and drained the bottle. When I finished

I grabbed another. I already felt a little looser.

"You can do this," Jamie said. "You know the lyrics, the changes, the structure. Hell, you helped to write some of these songs, Kallie."

It was true. I often gave Jamie sheets of lyrics and poems to use for the band's songs.

"Yeah," I said. "But I never thought I'd be singing them."

Just then I heard LeeLee pluck the low string on her bass, and the sound filled the store with a deep resonance that seemed to cut right through me.

I watched the girls with their various instruments, swiftly plugging in patch cords, using electronic tuners, switching on pedals, adjusting gain and volume and getting ready.

I watched as Jamie sat behind her drum kit, rapped her snare and tapped her foot against her kick pedal.

"Kallie," Jamie called, motioning with her drumstick. "You're up."

She pointed to a position in the center of the group, where a single microphone stood gleaming on its stand.

I walked over as if in a daze. I had never been in this position before, my back to the band and looking outward. It felt powerful to have my friends with all their electric power and energy standing behind me and backing me up.

"I don't know what to do," I said.

"Hang on," said Dolly. She leaned over and switched on the PA.

The sound in front of me changed, and I realized it was the monitor at my feet picking up the ambient noise near the mic. It hovered in front of my face.

"Give it a try," said LeeLee. "Just say something so we can check your levels."

"Um," I said and then jumped when I heard my disembodied voice echo around the room.

Dolly fiddled with the controls.

"Again," LeeLee said, encouraging me.

"Hi," I said shyly, and my voice came back to me louder than before. Dolly must have turned it up.

"We'll have to keep her cranked for now," said Dolly to Jamie. "She's probably mic-shy."

"What's that?" I asked, away from the microphone.

Dolly walked up to me with her guitar slung over her shoulder. It afforded her a sexy swagger that I had always envied. She gently pushed me closer to the mic.

"Grab it," she said and placed my hand on the mic. "You have to swallow the thing."

I rolled my eyes. "Get lost."

"No, seriously, Kallie. You need to get really close, so that you're touching it with your lips, and then you need to really push your air out. Everyone has a hard time at first, before they get used to it. The ones who can't get past it have a permanent case of the mic-shies."

"You got to give it everything, okay?" said Jamie. "Really let it rip. Loud."

LIVE LOUD.

My dad's note came back to me in my mind. Well, I was pretty sure this wasn't what he had meant, but it definitely applied. Besides, Dad had always wanted to pursue music as a career.

"Kallie?" Jamie said softy. "You okay?"

I shook my head as if to clear it. "Yeah," I said, this time into the microphone, and my voice came back to me like an affirmation.

Then I had a moment of inspiration. "Hey, how do I make my voice echo more? You know, like my name."

Dolly laughed. "You do already have a pretty kick-ass rock name, Miss Echo, but what you are referring to is reverb, and it's an effect that we can play around with later. For now, let's focus on the basics, okay?"

"Okay," I said, feeling a little more relaxed. The two beers I'd downed had helped things, I was sure.

"Let's start with 'Misery,'" said Jamie.

I waved her off. "No," I said. "I don't want to do that one right now. I don't want to feel like an imitator. Can't we just, um, jam?"

"She's right," said Dolly. "She's got to find her own voice."

The others agreed.

"Okay," said Jamie. "I'll start a rhythm and we'll find a groove. You come in with something when you get a feel for it, okay?"

I nodded and then cracked another beer. I was getting drunk, but I didn't care. I needed the courage, and it made me feel safer to have something besides the microphone in my hand.

Jamie kicked off, starting out with a slow, groovy beat, and then LeeLee joined in with a dark, melodic bass line that I could feel in my back molars. Man, being so close to the monitors and the amps was intense. Dolly picked up on the notes LeeLee was playing with a bluesy chord progression, and soon I found myself swaying to the tune as Jelly accented the burgeoning song with her keys. It was like I could almost see the invisible colors the music created.

I started thinking about my dad again, how young he was when he died, how painful it must have been for him to leave this world. To leave me. In the final days before he passed, when he was too weak to do anything except lie in his bed at the hospice, and his body had swelled up and his skin had cracked open, he had tried so hard to be brave.

As I stood at the microphone, I tried to breathe through the ache in my throat, and I wiped my nose with the back of my hand. The music was haunting, sad, dirgelike, and it was the kind of music I imagined being played at some Dark Ages funeral. I opened my mouth, not sure what might come out, not sure what I was going to sing.

I screamed.

It scared me at first—the sound and its ferocity, its desperation. And it felt good. So I screamed again, louder. And again, until I was screaming along with the music. Eventually my screams gave way to syllables that formed into a kind of wild, grief-stricken poem. I had always been good at making up poems on the fly.

I couldn't feel anything except the music and my own voice leaving my body. I wasn't Kallie anymore. I wasn't sure who I was exactly. I was someone who was tuned into the divine vibration of music. That magic place in between the notes and the melody. The sheer volume of my voice shocked me. I sang my heart out.

After a while I began to calm, the tempo slowed, and the song—or whatever it was we had just created— churned out its final notes.

Then…silence.

I was buzzing all over. My body, my head. My throat was sore from screaming, and my lungs felt as though they had had the best workout of my life. With trembling hands I released the microphone stand and unfurled my fists. I hadn't realized I'd been clenching it so hard. I was covered in sweat, even though I hadn't been dancing or even moving much. I shivered and looked around at the girls, seeing them as if for the first time. They were staring at me, awestruck and maybe a little concerned.

"Well," said Dolly, breaking the silence. "One thing is for sure. We are gonna have to turn her way down."

"No shit!" said LeeLee, wide-eyed. "I've never heard anything like that before."

"It was…" began Jelly. "Crazy," she said finally.

I looked to Jamie, who could always be counted on to tell me the truth. She was staring at me with a look I had never seen before. It was like she was seeing me for the first time too—and liked what she saw.

"Jamie," I said tentatively. "What do you think?" My voice was back to sounding like me—regular, quiet Kallie.

"Kalliope Echo," said Jamie. "Welcome to the band."

Everyone whooped, and I couldn't help but grin.

"Does this mean I get to go on tour?" I asked.

"Of course," said Dolly. "You're our front woman."

"Good," I said. "Because I won't have anywhere to live pretty soon."

That kind of killed the good cheer among the group for a minute as they all realized my situation.

"But there's a problem," said Jelly in typical downer fashion. "We can't be Fractured anymore. We have to change the name. Make a fresh start. New singer, new music, new name."

All the others nodded in agreement.

"Any ideas, Kallie?" asked Jamie.

I shrugged. I didn't care. I was just happy to be in the band.

"I know," said Dolly. "The perfect name. We should call ourselves Misery Girl, after Kallie. She came along and saved us with that crazy voice. It's an awesome name too."

"I like it," said Jamie. "All in favor?"

LeeLee and Jelly approved. Here I was, taking on the role of lead singer, and now the band was going to be named after me too. What if I let them all down?

As if she could read my mind, Jamie reassured me yet again. "What do you have to lose, Kallie? Without you, there is no band and no tour anyway. Let's try, okay?"

I looked at my friends. I saw their expectant faces and the belief they had in me.

"Let's do it," I said. "Let's try."

As they hooted and hollered, I tried to contain my joy but couldn't. I laughed and celebrated along with them. Despite the rough start, it ended up being a pretty great birthday. I had started with nothing and then gained a band. My band. Misery Girl.

Chapter Three

Jamie wanted to jam night and day. I didn't really have anything else to do anyhow. I would go over to the store every morning, and when Jamie dropped me off at my soon-to-be-ex-house every night, I would stumble in, scrape something to eat from the near-bare pantry and fall into bed. I had no time for laundry or daily chores.

One morning I could barely stand the smell of all of the clothes I picked up, so I raided my dad's closet. He had a faded purple Hendrix shirt that I loved. As I reached for it, a note fluttered down from the top shelf like a yellow, stiff-winged butterfly. As always, when I found echoes from my dad, my heart leaped with excitement. On the paper was a drawing of a star. And my dad's chicken-scratch handwriting:

Kallie, did you know that deep in space there is a giant star named Lucy? It is a crystallized diamond, actually floating out there in space. Isn't that neat? I told your mother this once too, when I proposed. I used my grandmother's ring. Did I ever show that to you? I can't remember. It's yours now. It's in the spot.
Dad

That was it. A diamond ring? No, he most certainly had not ever told me about that or shown me it. Maybe it was a delusion. Just before he died, he'd told me all kinds of tall tales that were certain to be pure fantasy, like having been at Woodstock or having met Eric Clapton. He was too young for any of that, after all.

Where was the spot he was talking about? We didn't have a "spot" in our house. Or did we? I sort of remembered him showing me some old letters once that he kept up on the top shelf with the books in the living room. Maybe it was there?

I ran out and grabbed the step stool. I had packed up a lot of the books already, but there were still so many to do, and I hadn't gotten to the ones up high yet. Just as I was about to dismiss the shelf and all the stuffy college literature anthologies on it, my fingers

happened to brush against cool metal.
A hexagonal tin. It was an old tea tin.
I carefully lifted it down and sat with
it on the floor.

Just then I heard Jamie pull up
outside and lay on the horn. I ignored
her. My fingers trembled around the
rim of the tin. I almost didn't dare open
it, but I had to. Carefully I flipped up
the lid. Inside were a lot of yellowed
envelopes and slips of paper. I took
the first one off the top. It was a piece
of cereal box, and it had three words
written on it in shaky script:

I LOVE YOU

That's all it said. I knew it was from
my dad to me and that he must have
written it during his final days at home.
I felt tears starting and hastily brushed
them away when I heard Jamie come up
to the door.

"Hey, Kallie," she called. "You better
not still be asleep." She opened the door

into the little room and saw me sitting there crying, with the tin in my lap.

"Echoes?" she asked.

I nodded and sniffled a reply. "Mmm-hmm."

"Have you had breakfast?" she asked.

I shook my head.

"Come on then," she said. "I'm taking you for pancakes."

I closed the tin, vowing to go through it carefully later, and placed it back up on the shelf. I took the piece of cardboard and placed it in my pocket. That one I would carry with me. I never wanted to let that one go.

Over breakfast Jamie was unusually quiet. There was something odd about her demeanor, and I couldn't figure out what it was. I thought maybe she was nervous about the tour. We had all been working so hard, and she'd been planning the logistics with military precision.

I had been worried she was getting obsessed.

"Kallie," she said after a while. "I have something to tell you."

The way she spoke sent chills up my spine. Instantly I had images of her telling me that she, too, was dying of cancer or that she was leaving me in some other way. I felt panic rise in my chest.

Noting my expression, she reached out a hand to reassure me. "It's not bad," she said. "Well, maybe it could be, depending on how you feel about it."

"What is it, Jamie?" I asked.

"I'm…I'm transitioning," she said and looked down at her hands.

At first I didn't know what to say, like my brain didn't compute, and then I understood. Jamie, my Jamie, was going to be male. And when I understood that, it seemed like the most natural thing in the entire world.

"Okay," I said, thinking there was more.

"What do you think?" she asked nervously.

"I think that's…I mean…I think it's great if you're happy."

"Yeah, I am," she said. "It feels good to finally be who I have always been inside. It's still a little confusing though, and the hormones kind of make me feel strange."

"Hormones? Wow, I didn't realize you had gotten that far." Something dawned on me. "Are you changing your name? Do you want me to refer to you as *he*?"

"No, and yes," Jamie answered. "I'm still going to go by Jamie. That's cool. But I want to be a *he*—I *am* a he," he corrected himself.

"I'm proud of you, you know. That takes guts. I don't know if I could ever be so brave."

"Thanks, Kallie. It means a lot coming from one of the bravest people I know."

I smiled at him. "Are we going to cry now? Have a Hallmark moment?"

Jamie laughed. "I'm a dude. I don't cry, remember?"

"Not if you're Robert Smith, you don't."

"Ah, a Cure reference. Nice."

And just like that we slipped back into our easy rapport. There wasn't a person on earth I felt more comfortable around than Jamie, and I felt honored that he had told me his news.

We ate the last of our pancakes with gusto, inspired by Jamie's courage and newfound excitement for the future. I didn't tell him about the ring in my dad's note, but I figured there was a time for everything.

Chapter Four

At our next gig we took pity on the
band that opened for us, an all-boy emo
group named SOFTFOCUS, and we
shared our beer. A couple of them were
kind of cute, and Dolly went a little nuts
for their singer, Damien. She started
drawing intersecting *D*s on her arm in
black lipstick. He seemed into her too,
and they disappeared into the gear room

together several times over the course of the night.

After our show, I wanted to blow off steam and do some more drinking, so we all lingered at the bar after hours with Damien and the drummer from SOFTFOCUS, a shaggy-haired guy named Adam.

Adam had this sweet way of peeking at me from under his bangs. He didn't exactly try to hide his admiring glances, which I found endearing, but he was still pretty shy. He made me feel like some sort of exotic creature that he was coveting.

Dolly and Damien were sucking face, Jelly was sleeping in the van outside, LeeLee was hanging with me and Adam, and Jamie was going over the set list from the show we had just done. He was noting mistakes and changes he wanted to make later on. I knew that after everyone else was asleep, he'd want to go over it all again. I smiled to myself. He was so passionate.

Jamie looked up from across the room and saw me smiling at him. He seemed surprised, and then he cracked his usual disarming grin. That was my Jamie, slaying everyone.

"What?" he mouthed at me, drowned out by the music.

I just shook my head and smiled.

I saw him get up and go to the bathroom, taking his leather hip pack with him. He always had it, and even though we didn't talk about it, I knew why. It contained his medication, the stuff he was using during his transition. He seemed so much happier, so much more like himself now.

After a while I was alone with Adam, and somehow his hand was up my shirt and his mouth was all over me. I found myself daydreaming while he touched me, and I couldn't get Jamie's smile out of my head. Every time I pictured him, I'd get a little rush of excitement. It was hot—and confusing.

Later that night Jamie was nowhere to be found, and the other girls had crashed out in the van. I tried to wait up for him but fell into a deep sleep.

I dreamed about my mother. I had told my friends she left when I was a baby, but that wasn't true. She left when I was a kid. I think she had some better idea for her life. Dad told me she had a lot of problems, but I didn't care. She still left. I couldn't forgive that.

Chapter Five

Over breakfast at our next stop, Jamie wouldn't meet my gaze. I raised my eyebrows at Dolly, who just shrugged.

Dolly wasn't her usual upbeat self. She just picked at her sausage.

"You okay?" I asked her.

She nodded. "Just not hungry. Hung over, I guess."

"So what's next?" I asked, expecting Jamie to chime in with our itinerary. He remained silent.

"Uh," said LeeLee, filling in the silence, "we have a pretty big gig at the university tonight. Big crowd. Sold out. Should be awesome."

"Okay," I said. "Jamie, do you want to go over the set list?"

Jamie gave me a withering stare. "Why?" he asked. "You seem to have everything figured out just fine." He pushed his plate away and got up to leave.

"What the hell?" I asked after he was gone.

I looked at Dolly and LeeLee and Jelly, who just stared at me.

"You know," LeeLee said gently, "for a sensitive person, you don't have a lot of insight."

"What do you mean?"

"Hello? He's in love with you. Always has been, always will be."

It was like someone stopped the great big turntable in the sky at that exact moment and the world stood still. Jamie in love with me?

"Um, excuse me, guys," I said and got up from the table.

As I walked outside toward Jamie, who was leaning against the van reading, I started to get kind of mad. It was just like Jamie to be angry with me for something I didn't even know about.

I walked up to him expecting a fight, but when I got closer I could see that he was crying. His eyes looked bluer than I had ever seen before, and the sight stopped me in my tracks.

He hastily wiped his eyes.

"Kallie," he said, "I'm sorry about that. I didn't have any right to think you were mine. But when I saw you with that drummer, Adam, the other night,

I just flipped out. I even went around punching things."

"Why didn't you say anything?"

"I just wish you had chosen maybe a bass player or something," he said. "Not another drummer. Not one who's better than me. Not one who has a…you know."

"Oh," I said quietly. This was making a lot more sense. I took a step forward, and he leaned back against the van, wary of what I might say.

"First of all," I said, "Adam is not the better drummer. You are. Second, he was nice, but I was drunk that night. One-time thing."

I reached over and took his hand and brought it up to my lips. I kissed his knuckles, and he gasped.

"What are you doing?" he whispered.

"Finding out for sure," I said.

I stepped forward, pressing my body against his. I felt him tense up and then relax as I took his face in my hands. I lifted my lips to his and kissed him.

It wasn't amazing. It wasn't fireworks. It wasn't like the movies. But it was right. Kissing Jamie felt so, so right.

When I pulled away, his eyes were still closed. "Wow," he whispered.

"How do you like me now?" I asked.

He smiled. "I love you, Kallie."

"You know this is a bad idea, right?" I asked. "The drummer and the lead singer hooking up?"

"Whatever," he said. "Maybe it's the best thing we ever did."

I laughed. "Yeah, maybe it is."

I slipped my hand into his and pulled him back toward the restaurant. I was hungry.

After we ate, Jamie and I sat nestled in the booth, nursing a couple of coffees. He kept one hand on my knee while he checked his phone for social-media updates or other news about our band.

Truthfully, I was kind of blissed out on my new boyfriend.

"Oh no," I said, realizing something.

"What?" asked Jamie.

"What if I can't write any good songs now?"

"What do you mean?" He frowned.

"I'm happy, so maybe I can't write rock songs now. Our music is about pain, right?"

Jamie laughed. "I'm sure you'll figure something out."

Jamie was a really sweet boyfriend. He was always holding doors open for me and giving me the pickles off his burger and stuff like that. After I confessed to him that I'd never received a valentine from a boy, he went out to a dollar store late at night, scored several of those kids' packs of valentines and addressed each and every one of them to me.

There must have been a hundred of those things. He hid them in my backpack, in my clothes, around the van, in my gear. It was like his own sweet version of an echo. Every time I opened something, I would find one, or it would flutter out of nowhere, a sweet little card with teddy bears and hearts drawn on it.

For a little while everything seemed right with the world.

Chapter Six

"I've got some great news," said Jamie. "A manager named Mike Michaelson contacted us and wants to meet up. He secured us a gig at the Ballroom, no finder's fee. This could be it, Kallie."

"Wow," I said. This was crazy timing. "That's great."

"The booker fronted us fifty percent of our fee. A thousand bucks. That's the biggest payout yet. I think we should get ourselves into a hotel. And make it a nice one. Maybe order room service. It's been a long time since we had a decent meal, and you are all getting too skinny."

We laughed.

"Sounds good," I said. Honestly, I needed a rest. I had been burning out for a while, and with all the drama I was starting to crash. I wasn't sure how much more I could take. The new big gig and interest from a manager was exciting, but it was also a lot of pressure.

As soon as we signed with Mike, Jamie had us in the van and on the way to a studio to record. Our band pulled up to a large brick building, and we tumbled out. We had started to unload our gear when Mike popped his head out of the heavy metal door on the side of the building.

"Hey!" he called. "We've got all that in here. Dolly, LeeLee, just bring your guitars. Jamie, bring your snare and your sticks if you want. Anj, Misery, we've got everything you need."

I kind of liked how Mike insisted on calling me Misery, but I could tell that it kind of bugged Jamie. He rolled his eyes at me.

"Come on, Misery," said Jamie. "Destiny awaits."

The girls grabbed their guitars and Jamie his sticks, and we went in through the heavy door.

It was like walking into a musician's wet dream. There was a soundproof studio, set up with every instrument we could need, and a full control panel and editing station that we couldn't possibly hope to understand. The place was decorated with endless posters, autographs, handbills and vintage vinyl records. My dad would have loved it there. I felt a pang of loneliness for him but decided it was best to just suck it up and get the most out of the experience, for his sake. After all, he had said I should *live loud*.

Mike motioned to a shabby-looking couch, and we all plopped down and waited.

A few seconds later a short fellow with a receding hairline came out of a side room and hurried toward us.

"Hey," he said. "I'm Johnny Pop. Nice to meet you. Why don't you guys go get set up and we'll get some levels, okay?"

I nodded, pretending I understood what the hell he was talking about, and went to follow the band into the main room.

"Misery. You're in there," he said, pointing to a small soundproof booth next to the main studio. "The singer's closet," he said.

That was weird. I had never sung separately from the band before. I wasn't sure I could do it without them.

"But," I said, feeling the nerves kick in, "we play live. I mean, I always sing with them. How will I hear?" As soon as I said it, I knew it was a rookie's question.

Johnny, to his credit, did not try to make me feel like an amateur. He simply held up a pair of headphones for me to take. I was liking him more and more.

"You'll be able to hear them, and me and yourself, with these," he said. "Don't worry—it will feel strange at first, but you'll get the hang of it."

"Oh," I said, taking the headphones.

I opened the booth and stepped inside. I was expecting it to feel like a shower or something, but it was actually really cozy and calming.

Johnny opened the door and adjusted the mic for me so that it was level with my face.

"Here," he said, producing a silver flask. "This will warm you up. Just don't make it a habit, okay? Not good for the throat."

I grinned and took a swallow. It was good. I went to give it back to him, but he motioned for me to keep it. So I did.

He shut the door, and a few seconds later the lights inside dimmed. I placed the headphones on and heard a faint crackle, then the sound of Johnny's voice.

"How you doing, Misery?"

"Good," I said, leaning toward the mic.

"Don't lean in—don't strain. Just be natural, and the booth will capture it. All right now, Misery. The band is ready. In a moment you'll hear me count them in, and then they'll start the track. You come in on your cue."

"Okay," I said.

After a moment I heard Johnny count down from five, and then I heard the sharp crack of Jamie's sticks against the snare. A second later I heard Dolly and LeeLee join in. After that Jelly began her melody. Wow, it sounded incredible. So incredible that I got wrapped up in listening and missed my cue.

"Cut!" Johnny's voice came in and the music stopped. "Misery, you okay?"

"Y-yeah, sorry," I said. I took another drink. "I'm good now. Let's go."

Another take kicked off, followed by another screwup by Yours Truly.

After yet another failed attempt, I heard Jamie's voice. "Hey, can we try something?" he asked.

"Sure," said Johnny.

"Hey, Kallie," said Jamie. "Let's do 'The Way Things Used to Be.' What do you say?"

"The Way Things Used to Be" was a new song Jamie and I had been working on. It was about my mom, and even though the band had been tinkering with it, I hadn't fully opened up and sung the whole thing through yet.

"Okay," I said.

Then I understood why Jamie thought it was a great idea. The song started and ended with me. The band came in after I sang the first line. Clever Jamie, always looking out for me.

"Um, Johnny, I start on this one," I said into the mic.

"Great, Misery. I'll count you down and then you start."

"Okay," I said and took a deep breath. I needed full lungs for this one. It was epic in volume, and it was a song that took a lot out of me, both vocally and emotionally.

I heard Johnny count down, and then I opened my mouth and sang. After I finished, there was a moment of silence, and then I heard a quiet "wow" come through the headset. It was Johnny.

"Okay?" I asked, breathless.

"Goose bumps, baby," said Johnny. "Now I've got to get the parts from the other players and put it together. We might need to come back and loop over some spots later, okay?"

"Okay," I said. "Can I come out?"

"You bet. Come watch the magic."

I exited the booth and saw Mike staring at me with dollar signs in his eyes.

I watched through the studio window as Jamie adjusted the drum kit. He looked up and gave me a thumbs-up and his dazzling smile.

I smiled back and blew him a kiss of luck. He pretended to grab it and placed it on his cheek. He was so cute, it was disgusting.

"Ah, I see," said Johnny, not unkindly. "Romeo and Juliet."

"More like Sid and Nancy, minus the heroin," said Dolly as she exited the room.

"Neither," I said. "Dallas Winston and Cherry Valance."

Mike raised an eyebrow. "Don't know them."

"Ah, yes," said Johnny. "*Outsiders*! Patrick Swayze's my jam," he explained.

It was official—I really, really liked Johnny. I sat down next to him in the booth.

"What's next?" I asked.

"Well, I'm going to get Jamie to play that same track again, and I'm going to lay down the drum track. He'll have to play to a click so we can get a tight base to work from."

"A click?" I asked.

"Like a metronome," explained Mike. "As the drummer, he needs to be perfectly in time or else it will be impossible to mix together the other tracks properly. It won't sound right."

"Ah," I said. "Is that hard?"

Johnny nodded, fiddling with controls. "It can be very challenging," he said. "Especially for drummers who are not classically trained and who are used to playing live."

Uh-oh, I thought. That sounded like Jamie. He was totally self-taught.

"Well, couldn't we just record our live sound?" asked Dolly.

"Yes, you could," said Johnny. "But it's better to do a studio album. It's the difference between Nirvana *Unplugged* and *In Utero*."

I watched as Jamie adjusted his headphones and got ready. Johnny counted him down and Jamie had no sooner gotten started than Johnny yelled, "Cut," and he had to start again. That happened at least five times in a row.

I cringed. I could tell Jamie was getting frustrated. He was a perfectionist. There wasn't anything I could do to help him, so I just had to watch and wait. After what seemed like an eternity, Jamie managed to get midway through the song.

Then he got three-quarters of the way through. By the time he managed to play through to the ending, the other girls were asleep on the couch and I was ready to find a new profession.

"Is it usually like this?" I asked Johnny.

He laughed. "Not as glamorous as you thought, hey? Well, that's the gig. It's a long process, but it's worth it. Wait until you guys hear the completed track. Don't worry—the rest will go quicker now that we have the drums down."

"Okay, guys, why don't you go grab some food and take a break. I'll have an early mix for you soon. It won't be fully mastered, but at least you'll have something to think about."

"Thanks, Johnny," I said.

"Yeah, thanks," said Jamie. "It has been a real honor to work with you. I really learned a lot."

"Hey, no problem, kid. Watch out, or you'll give me a fat head." Johnny reached out and shook Jamie's hand.

"Mike, you coming?" Dolly called as we filed out to the van.

"No, sweetheart, I'm going to stay and work on this with Johnny."

"Okay," she said.

"We'll bring you back a doggie bag," said LeeLee.

As we walked to the van, I felt like I was floating on air. That was intense. It was awesome. I could tell everyone else was feeling it too, because no one could stop grinning. "Where to?" Jamie asked.

"Steak," said Jelly.

"Japanese," said Dolly.

"Salad," said LeeLee.

"Whatever," I said. "Food. And something to drink." And then I remembered I still had Johnny's flask.

"Hang on a sec," I said to Jamie as I popped out of the van. "I have to return this."

I ran back to the studio, a chorus of groans and complaints floating after me.

I opened the door and walked in. Mike and Johnny were at the controls, having a heated discussion.

"Look, Mike, I think you're being rash. Yes, the kid had trouble with the click track, but he's got talent. Don't ruin it by getting greedy."

"Yeah," said Mike, "but drummers like him are a dime a dozen. Hell, the whole band could probably be scrapped, save for that hot guitarist and Misery, of course. Let's face it—she's the real deal. She's the Courtney Love of the outfit. The rest can go. Frankly, I don't know if the market is ready for whatever that Jamie kid is."

I had heard enough. The sheer gall this joker had to lie to our faces and then rip us apart as soon as we were out of earshot enraged me.

"What. The. Hell!" I yelled.

Mike and Johnny jumped, spinning around in their seats to see me standing there, red-faced and wielding Johnny's silver flask.

"You snake!" I was seething. I think I was literally seeing red.

"Whoa there, Kallie," said Mike, standing up.

"You should be ashamed of yourself," I said. I was so mad I felt like I was going to cry. I most definitely did not want to do that.

"Kallie, look, this isn't something unheard of. Lots of times you get a band and there are a couple of talented members and the rest are…well, they're fine, but they're holding the stars back, you know?"

He leaned in closer to me.

"Besides," he said. "You're a star, Kallie. The others…not so much.

Don't you want to be famous? Don't you want to make enough money to pay rent? Huh? Jamie told me about your dad and everything."

At that moment, as he mentioned my dad and my old house, I felt something crack in my mind. I could almost hear it happening. It was the sound of me completely and totally losing it.

"SCREW YOU!" I screamed as I nailed him across the temple with Johnny's silver flask.

Mike's head snapped backward, and he staggered away from me, his hand on his head.

I could see blood seeping out from between his fingers.

"You bitch!" He lunged at me.

"No!" Johnny jumped in front of me, blocking me, and gave Mike a swift jab to the solar plexus. Mike went down, hard.

"Oh shit," I said, suddenly scared. I had never really hit anyone before.

As wild as I could be onstage, I didn't really believe in violence. And as much as I hated Mike's guts, I felt terrible that I had caused him an injury.

"Don't worry," said Johnny. "I'll take care of him. You get out of here. I'm going to make some calls to a few friends, and Mike here will be riding out of town on whatever bus he rode in on."

"But…" I trailed off, pointing to Mike's head.

"It's not that bad," said Johnny. "Besides, it was my flask that did it."

"Sorry," I said.

"It's okay. Get out of here."

I ran out the door.

Everyone was pissy with me when I got back because I had taken so long, and I didn't have the heart to tell them what had happened. Jamie gave me a look, as if he knew something was up, but I was too mad at him to even speak. He had told Mike about me, about my life and my dad. He had told him about my homelessness, for crying out loud. Where did he get off?

Why was it that when something good happened in my life, it almost always got ruined before I had a chance to enjoy it? Couldn't I for once just have a moment to be happy? Why did I keep losing everything that mattered to me? At dinner I ignored my food and just drank.

I wondered if my whole life was going to be this roller coaster of ups and downs. Was it me? Or was I just unlucky?

"Do you think I see things wrong?" I slurred at the waiter.

He just looked at me quizzically.

"More beer?" he asked.

I shook my head. I was dizzy.

"Water," I said weakly. I stood up to go to the bathroom and promptly fell on my face. I considered trying to get up for a moment, but it was too much effort. Instead, I made friends with the carpet and succumbed to a blackness of sleep.

Chapter Seven

I woke up back at the hotel, my head pounding. Someone had removed my jeans and boots and had plopped me onto the loveseat. I was alone. Everyone must have been at breakfast.

I groaned. When the band came back I would have to tell them about Mike. I would have to confront Jamie about his big mouth too. I needed a shower first.

Gingerly I picked myself up off the loveseat. I went into the big sparkling bathroom and turned on the hot water.

I peeled off my T-shirt, undies and bra and stepped under the spray. Man, that felt good. I felt my shoulders relax and wrapped my arms around myself in a kind of hug. The warmth enveloped me, and it was my undoing. I began to cry. Not just a small cry either—a big cry. A from-the-bottoms-of-your-feet kind of cry. It hurt and felt good all at once. I cried the way I should have when my dad died. I cried the way I should have when my mom left.

I heard the door latch click, and then someone walked into the bathroom. It was Jamie.

"Babe?" he called, his voice full of concern.

"Y-yeah?" I sniffled, but I was no longer sad. In fact, I was happy to hear his voice. I could forget all that bullshit about him talking to Mike about me. He was probably just worried in typical Jamie fashion. I was lucky to have someone who cared so much about me.

I peeled back the curtain a bit and poked my head out. I might have even let the shower curtain reveal a little more.

Jamie blushed, and I smiled. A tiny victory. I figured I'd make my revenge the sexy kind. Then we'd both have fun.

"Uh," he said, trying to tear his eyes from me and failing, "you okay?"

"Yeah," I said. "You?"

"Yeah."

"Want to come in?" I asked.

Again he blushed. "Yes," he whispered. "But..."

"But what?" I asked and then wished I hadn't. I knew why. He didn't want me to see him. Jamie was always hiding his body.

I had an idea. "Turn off the light," I said.

"What?"

"Turn it off and get in here."

Jamie's eyes widened. "Okay," he said.

A second later the light went out, and it was almost totally dark in the bathroom. I felt the curtain shift and then sensed Jamie's body come closer to mine. He stood just beyond my reach.

"Come here," I said softly.

I felt him inch forward, and when he was close enough I took him in my arms and held him against me under the spray of the shower. He was trembling, but I just ran my hands up and down his back, caressing him as the warm water washed over us.

"This is nice," I murmured.

"Mmm," said Jamie. "Will you hold me like this forever?"

I sighed and held him a little tighter. We stayed like that until the water began to run cold.

I let him get out first so he could quickly dress. As much as I wanted to see him, I didn't want to rush him. I figured he'd show me when he was ready. I could wait. Something told me I'd have a lifetime with him.

He looked up at me as he ran a towel across his short hair. "What?" he asked.

"I love you," I said.

Jamie smiled, and I knew I could never get sick of that sight.

"This is turning into a great day," Jamie said. "After last night I thought you were mad at me for something. I thought maybe you were disappointed in my drum performance."

"What? No, Jamie, that's not…oh man. I have something to tell you."

"What is it?"

I stepped out of the shower and began drying off. Jamie handed me my clothes.

"Um. I have bad news. It's Mike. I, uh, fired him."

"You WHAT?" Jamie was beyond shocked. "Why in the hell would you do that?"

"Let me explain," I said. "He wanted to split up the band. I heard him talking about us when I went back into the studio, and what he was saying was, well, less than flattering. He was bad news."

"Shit," said Jamie. "Are you sure?"

"Yeah," I said. "I'm sorry. But it's better that we find out now."

Jamie nodded. "What do we tell the girls?"

Just then the bathroom door flung open to reveal Dolly, LeeLee and Jelly. They looked downtrodden, heartbroken.

"Whoa," I said. "I guess you guys heard us."

Jelly nodded. "Screw that Mike guy. I didn't like him anyway. Plus, his first name and last name were too similar. Creepy."

"Yeah, whatever," said Dolly.

"Good riddance," said LeeLee.

But their faces betrayed them. They all seemed really sad. Dolly in particular was looking at me with a grave expression. There was something else. I was scared to ask. Fortunately, Jamie did it for me.

"You guys," he said. "What's going on? What's wrong?"

"I'm sorry, Kallie," said Dolly. "We tried to make her go away."

"Huh?" I asked. What were they talking about? Who?

"Who?" asked Jamie, echoing my thoughts.

In a horrible moment of clarity, an image flashed in my mind.

"No, Dolly," I said. "Don't. Don't say it."

"I'm sorry, Kallie. Your mom is here."

In what seemed like the fundamental aspect of my existence, that great big turntable in the sky scratched and reversed again, and I was left reeling. Of course. Of course she would choose to show up now. Right before the biggest show our band had ever played. This was my moment, and she was here to ruin it.

"Baby," said Jamie. "You don't have to see her."

"No, I do," I said. I needed to see her, get it over with and move on with my life.

"She's in the lobby," said LeeLee.

"I'll go with you," offered Jelly. "I have some experience with messed-up moms."

I nodded. "I know. But I think I have to do this by myself."

"Okay," said Jamie. "Whatever you need."

"What I need is my dad," I said, and I felt the tears start to fall again.

"Honey," said Dolly, "you have a little piece of your dad right here."

I thought for a moment. Of course, she was right. The tea tin that contained Dad's echoes. I had been putting it off for so long.

"Yeah," I said. "You're right. Okay. I'll open the tin."

Dolly smiled. "That's my girl."

"We're going to head over to the studio to talk to Johnny," said LeeLee. "He called Dolly's cell a few minutes ago. He says we can come practice before the gig tomorrow. No Mike."

I nodded. "Okay," I said. "You guys go on ahead. I'll show up later."

They gathered their stuff to leave, and Jamie gave me a last look.

Once they were gone I pulled out the tea tin and sat down on the loveseat.

There were the random scraps of paper my dad had stashed for me, all his echoes and lost notes. I didn't know where to begin, so I started at the top.

I picked up a piece of thin lined paper and unfolded it. I recognized my dad's handwriting immediately. It was like getting a hug from him from across the universe. I read the echo:

Kalliope,

Did you know that Kalliope was the eldest of the muses? The muses were the goddesses of music.

I named you after her because I had never been that eloquent. All my life I tried to write songs and make it in music, but I just didn't have the talent. Then you were born. And I did my best writing every day since. Thank you for being my muse.

Love,

Dad

The tears were really flowing. But I couldn't stop. I opened another.

Baby girl,

In case you have the foolish idea that you were ever a mistake, or ever anything but a divine gift from the universe, you need to know that my life as your dad has been a great life.

Yes, honey, it was short. The end sucked. But I don't regret a single moment I spent with you.

Daddy

God, could I do this? I picked up an envelope labeled *MOM* and opened it, not sure what I'd find.

Kallie,

Your mom just left, and I don't know how or what to tell you. You're only a little girl, and you must be so hurt. I know I am.

Kallie, your mom does love you, but she has problems. Serious problems.

I hope one day she will come back and you will forgive her. I will try too.

Dad

PS. I love you more than anything. All the time. No matter what. And I will never leave you.

I sighed and leaned back on the loveseat. Dad did leave, but not by choice. And now the woman who abandoned us was back, waiting in the lobby right this moment.

I looked in the tin. There was one note left. I opened it.

LOVE.

Remember what is most important. LOVE, FRIENDS, FAMILY.

If you remember that, you cannot go wrong.

I have loved you every day of your life. I will love you until the end of time.

"Oh, Dad," I whispered. "I love you too."

I looked into the tin. Inside was a small purple velvet ring box. With shaking hands I lifted it out. I was scared when I opened it that it would be empty, but it wasn't.

Inside was an antique-looking ring with a diamond in the center and yellow stones on the outside. It looked like a starburst. I tried it on, but it was way too big.

I placed it on the chain I wore around my neck, next to one of Dolly's shredded guitar picks. I breathed in deeply. Time to go and meet the past.

Chapter Eight

The elevator ride down from the sixth floor was quick—too quick—and I wished it had given me more time to prepare. I felt myself slipping into Misery mode, but I squashed it down. If I was going to face my mom, I had to do it as Kallie, as myself.

But what if I did? What if I saw her and she was sorry and she wanted to be part of my life again? What then? The thought had me reeling, and a little hopeful too. I figured she'd sought me out because of the publicity the band had been getting and because of our upcoming show, but that only made her silence after dad's death all the more painful. Where was she then?

The elevator doors opened and I stepped into the lobby. At first I thought it was empty, but then I spotted a head of dark hair partly obscured by a potted plant. When I walked around the nicely upholstered couches and armchairs, I could see that it was a woman's.

She was very thin, with long black hair and a long face. It was Mom. Even though I hadn't seen her for half my life, I knew her instantly. It was almost like I could feel an invisible string drawing me to her, or an energy field that linked us together. As I stood and stared at her, she turned her head. She smiled.

I wanted to bolt and run out of there to go find Jamie, have him hold me and comfort me, but I knew I had to face her. Besides, she had seen me and was rising from her seat. Man, was she skinny. And she looked old, much older than Dad had looked, and they were the same age.

I had seen pictures of her as I was growing up—Dad would never have kept those from me, wouldn't have hurt me like that no matter how angry he was at her—and she looked like a shadow of her former self.

"Kalliope," she said, and her voice cut through me like a knife.

"Anna," I said, using her proper name, and I could see her smile falter a little bit. *See, Mom? I can cut too.*

"Please," she said. "Can we talk?"

I walked over to her, and my legs felt like they were made of lead. I got close enough to touch her, and when she held her arms out to me in an awkward attempt at a hug, I slipped past her and sunk down onto the couch.

"Okay," she said and sat down too.

"Hi," I said, feeling a little bolder.

"Hi," she said, almost shyly. She looked me over, taking me in, and I could tell she was sizing me up just as much as I was sizing her up.

I noticed that her hands looked rough, like they had been plunged into very hot water for many years, and all the veins stood out on her forearms. Her legs looked like sticks in her loose trousers. I could tell that if she weren't so wasted-looking, she'd be quite an attractive woman, beautiful even, but the lines in her face were unhappy lines, and her teeth were in horrible condition.

"Kalliope," she said, again insisting on using my full name, the name my dad had given me. "I have been following you and your band's progress."

She rummaged in her oversized bag and produced a couple of our handbills and gig posters.

"Wow," I said. I was surprised by the sound of my own voice. I sounded older, stronger and infinitely edgier than I'd thought I would.

"Okay," she said. "I get it. I haven't been around. But I'm so proud of you, Kalliope. Of what you've done. You've accomplished what even your dad could never do."

When she said that, it was like all the air was suddenly sucked from the room.

"Don't talk about him," I said through clenched teeth.

"Kalliope, I'm sorry that he passed. That must have been so hard for you."

"What do you know about it?" I wanted to scream the words, but instead they came out in this eerily calm way that freaked even me out.

I could see it unsettled her too. She shifted in her seat.

"You're right. I'm sorry."

"Yeah. You should be, you know? I was alone and he was dying."

"I'm here now," she said. She leaned in toward me. After a moment she pointed at my neck.

"What?" I asked.

"Is that…? No, it couldn't be. Is that my ring?"

I was speechless. I didn't know what to say. I gave a half nod.

"Wow, it's great that your dad kept it all this time. I kind of thought he'd lost it."

"No," I said. "He didn't lose it. He kept it. For me."

"You know, Kallie," she said, "I'm having a bit of a hard time right now. This is difficult for me to say, but I don't have anywhere to live. I lost my apartment."

"Homeless?" I asked. "I know something about that."

"Then you know how rough it is," she said. "I thought maybe you could give me a job with your band, or maybe loan me a few bucks. But now that I see you have my ring, maybe you can just give it back to me and I'll be out of your hair."

As I looked at her, a funny thing happened. A lot of my anger just kind of melted away. This wasn't about me. It wasn't about how much she loved me or didn't love me, or whether I was lovable enough. I knew that I was enough. I had proof of that in my dad and in my friends and in Jamie. I felt it within myself. This was about a sick woman looking to score.

Slowly I took the ring off my necklace and placed it in her open palm. She snatched her hand away after our brief touch, the only touch we'd had in so many years, and immediately began inspecting the ring. I knew she'd pawn it the first chance she got.

"It's yours." I shrugged. "With one catch," I added.

She looked at me expectantly. "Yes?"

"We're done after this. I don't want to hear from you again."

"Oh," she said, unfazed. "Okay, no problem." I knew then that she thought I had done her a favor. A payday with no strings attached. But look at what she was giving up.

"Goodbye," I said.

"Goodbye."

I got up and walked out of the hotel and onto the street. I did not look back. The past was inside. My future was somewhere on the road ahead.

Chapter Nine

I heard the sounds of the band from outside the studio, and the familiar chord progressions and rhythms were a relief to me.

I pushed open the heavy door and went inside. Jamie was sitting at the controls with Johnny, deep in excited conversation, when he saw me and leaped up.

"Kallie," he said. He rushed over. "You okay?"

I nodded. "Yeah," I said. "Yeah, it was okay."

"So? What happened?"

"Well, I saw her. She was a sad, lonely person. I gave her back her ring—the one from the tin Dad left me—and I said goodbye. She's gone."

"Why did you give her the ring? Wasn't that supposed to be for you?"

I shrugged. "It was just a thing," I said. "And I didn't even lay eyes on it until today."

Jamie leaned in and hugged me tightly.

"Okay," he said, letting me go. "What do you want first? The good news or the great news?" he asked.

I laughed. "Um, all of it, I guess."

"Well, that dipshit Mike leaked our raw track to the Internet last night."

Reading my shocked expression, he quickly explained, "But it backfired, see? He thought it would be bad for us, but the song has taken off. It's practically gone viral!"

"It's not viral, Jamie, but it does have thousands of downloads," said Jelly from her perch in the corner. She was clicking away on the laptop, no doubt managing all our social-media sites at once.

"So anyway," said Jamie, rolling his eyes at Jelly, "the venue is sold out for tomorrow, and they've booked us for three more nights to accommodate the demand!"

"Awesome," I said.

"And that's not all," said Jamie. "Johnny wants to manage us. And he's the real deal."

"Yes!" I exclaimed. "Hell yes!"

I couldn't think of a better manager. He knew the music, the tech, he loved our sound, and he'd even saved me from that psycho Mike.

"The others?" I asked Jamie. "Are they in?"

"You bet," said Dolly, poking her head out of the studio door. "LeeLee's all over it."

"Yeah," said Johnny. "She's been up my butt all day about contracts."

I laughed. "That's our LeeLee."

"Well," said Johnny. "What are you waiting for, Misery?" He motioned to the vocal booth. "Ready to work out that big voice?"

I nodded. "Bring it," I said.

The inside of the recording booth felt like home. It was warm and cozy, and it felt good to open up and sing and release all my tension.

"What's next?" I asked.

"Well," said Johnny, "Jamie has something, uh, special to perform."

"Oh yeah?" I asked, intrigued. Jelly and LeeLee came out of the studio, and Jamie stayed behind with Dolly. I watched through the glass as he sat on a stool next to her and she picked up an acoustic guitar.

"Anytime you're ready, kid," said Johnny.

"This one is for Kallie," said Jamie into the mic. "It's called 'Another Miserable Love Song.'"

Dolly started picking a really haunting and pretty melody, and after a few bars Jamie started singing. I had never heard him sing before, not properly. He would sometimes sing along with me as we were working out songs, but not in full voice. He was actually pretty good, and I could hear how his voice had deepened lately.

He sang about wishing for me, about finding me and about never wanting to let me go.

Dolly strummed the final chords and then the studio was silent. I was crying. Jamie's song was so full of pain, and I knew it wasn't just a song about loving me. It was a song about me loving him.

I looked around and saw that everyone else was moved too.

Jelly sniffled. "Oh my god, you guys," she said. "I hope I fall in love with someone that way too."

"If I can, you can," said Jamie as he emerged from the studio. He walked over to me, took me in his arms and kissed me. It was a slow, deep kiss, and in it I felt everything he had sung about in his song.

"Did you like it?" he whispered as we came up for air.

"I loved it," I whispered back.

He smiled his dazzling Jamie smile, and I felt it light me up inside like it always did.

"I think it should be our first single," said Dolly. "It's not heavy like our other stuff, but it's beautiful, and I think it will get more radio play."

"Totally," said LeeLee. "I can hear that a simple, deep, Portishead-like bass line would go great with it."

"Yeah," said Jelly. "And I know exactly what to play over Dolly's melody."

"Kallie?" asked Jamie. "You want to sing this? I wrote it with you in mind. No one else can hit the full range of these notes."

"Only if you back me up," I said.

"That's a great idea," said Johnny. "It will add another layer to the song. Like a duet. Misery, get your butt in the booth and let's lay this down while the feelings are hot!"

"You got it," I said. I looked at Jamie. "Lyrics, babe?"

"Sure." He handed over a sheet and gave me a wink.

In a matter of moments we were deep into the process, trying out versions, adding parts, working out the kinks and laying down the track. It was amazing.

After such a productive session in the studio, we were all starving, so we went for steaks. "You guys," said Jelly, breaking the silence, "I'm kind of freaking out."

"Me too." Dolly sighed. "This gig is a big deal."

LeeLee put down her fork. "Listen, bitches," she said, and her tone shocked me. "We're not going to have any of this. It's just a gig. We go, we play our songs, we rock out, and we go home. Let's not puss out now."

I nodded. "You're right. We're Misery Girl. We're a punk band, for crying out loud. We don't buckle under pressure. Screw everyone else. We play for us. If they want to hate us, let them."

"Yeah!" said Dolly.

"Yeah," said Jelly. "Looks like someone already does." She was staring at her phone.

Uh-oh. "What?" I asked.

"An article is up on *Note for Note*'s blog. There's some hot shots of you, Kallie. And a few good quotes from Jamie, about him coming out as trans, but there's also some bullshit about death threats. What the hell is that?" Jelly looked up at me, scared.

I shook my head. "I don't know. Just rumors, I think. Where's Johnny?" I asked, but LeeLee had already pulled out her phone.

"Johnny," she said when she got him on the line, "what's this about...? Yeah, yeah? Okay. Yeah. Okay. Yes, we will. Thanks. Bye." She ended the call and looked at me. "Johnny says he's all over it, that it sounds like a meaning-less anonymous threat and we shouldn't let it get to us. He does want us to go straight back to the hotel after dinner, and he'll have a private security guard look out for us until after these shows are over. He says he had to negotiate, but the venue is paying for it. He told them we wouldn't play there without it."

"Okay," I said, feeling a bit more secure. "Let's just enjoy our food, and then we'll go back and get some rest."

"But first, a toast," said LeeLee, holding up a bottle of wine.

"Um, not for me," I said.

"Really?" she asked, incredulous.

"Yeah, after seeing my mom I just don't need to go there."

"You mean, you're going to sing sober?" asked Dolly.

"Yeah, why?" I asked, getting nervous.

"That's great!" she said. "Your voice is better when you're not drinking."

"Really?" I asked. "Why didn't you say something?"

Dolly shrugged. "I thought you'd figure it out in your own time."

"Yeah," I said. "Let's not do that anymore, okay? Let's not assume that we're all fine. From now on, let's check in."

Jelly nodded. "That sounds good to me."

"Me too," said LeeLee.

"You got it, girl," said Dolly. "I wouldn't know what I would do without you guys. You're my life."

"And you're mine," I said.

I looked around the table at them, at my girls, my band, my best friends. What a life it was.

Chapter Ten

When we got back to the hotel, Jamie wasn't there, Whatever, I thought. All I wanted was to crash.

I grabbed Jamie's Dead Kennedys hoodie, the one he had worn thin, and snuggled into it. I curled up on the sofa bed and drifted off.

Sometime later I heard a squeak and

rolled over to see Jamie sneaking into bed. It felt late.

"Jamie?" I murmured. "So late…"

"Yeah, baby," he said. "Go back to sleep. I'm here now."

He scooted over to me and took me in his arms, and I fell instantly back to sleep.

The morning was a blur. There were people everywhere. Our little band had somehow exploded into a giant crew of people, with Johnny leading the charge of a few hired roadies, reps from the venue and a few other people he had called in favors with to help us get ready and organized.

One of the men there, an impossibly tall dude named Jake, was our designated security force. He hovered around me relentlessly, and I swear he actually cast a shadow he was so tall. Dolly, LeeLee, Jelly and Jamie were all tinkering with their gear, making sure it was in working order and that they had backup.

I excused myself to the bathroom at the last minute and started my transformation into Misery. I had picked out my clothes the night before. I was going to wear my dad's old Nirvana T-shirt as a tribute, but instead of pairing it with jeans, I was going to wear it with a studded belt and tights, like a teeny minidress. When I put it on it was awfully short, but I just took a deep breath and willed myself not to care. Misery would not care. Then I took a pair of ripped fishnets and pulled them on over my tights. I slipped on my spike-heeled boots. They weren't great for walking, but they made me about four inches taller and were an instant confidence boost.

My hair, in a constant state of flux between black shoulder-length, shaggy bob and long pixie, was again getting too long. I grabbed a razor off the vanity and started chopping into it, shaving away some of the bulk and giving myself eye-skimming bangs. I messed it up with my hands. Not bad. I didn't ever wear much makeup, but onstage I needed more. I used some near-white concealer to make myself a little more pale—not super goth pale, just enough to look a little inhuman. Then I used black eyeliner to mark a straight black line underneath my eyes.

I emerged from the bathroom and everyone turned to look at me. I felt the energy shift. They were no longer looking at Kallie, and they knew it. They were staring at Misery.

"Well," I said, my voice already dropping into Misery's tone, "you guys coming or what?"

Jamie cracked a grin, and we all filed out the door and to the van.

"Nervous?" whispered Jamie. He and I were snuggled together in the back while Jake, the security guy, drove.

"Um, not really," I said. "Not about the gig." I pointed at Jake.

Jamie nodded. "Yeah, I'm sorry I didn't talk to you about that before. I didn't want to scare you. Just some nutcase on the Internet."

"Yeah," I said. "That's what everyone keeps saying." I paused. "Do me a favor?"

"Anything."

"Smile for me."

And he did. A genuine, true-blue Jamie dazzler. It was all I needed to carry me through.

The place was packed, thumping with aggressive teenage energy, and the time between acts flew by. We were up next, and the five of us waited in the wings backstage. Jake, ever present, hovered nearby. I turned to him.

"Um, dude, you going to come onstage with me?" I asked.

"No. This is where you leave me. We swept the venue. Everyone back here has credentials. You're good. I'll be watching from here."

"Okay," I said, somewhat reassured.

"You guys ready?" Dolly asked. She was almost humming with excitement.

We all nodded.

"You guys," said Jamie, "I just want you all to know that this has been the greatest time of my life. No matter what, I love you all, and I'm just really happy to be here with you."

"Aaw!" cooed LeeLee.

We all went in for a group hug.

The announcer took the stage and stepped up to the mic.

"PLEASE WELCOME TO THE STAGE…MISERY GIRL!"

The ensuing cheers and roaring applause and stomping were deafening as we ran onto the stage and took our places. The venue had been plunged into blackness, but I could find my way to my mic because the stage crew had pasted nifty pieces of glow tape all over the stage.

I stepped up to the mic. I could hear, even feel, the faint buzz of electricity that told me it was live. The monitors at my feet were huge.

I opened my mouth—Misery's mouth—and pressed my lips to the mic, kissing the crosshatched metal. I breathed in and could hear myself amplified through the monitors at my feet. A surge of power rose in my gut. I let the resulting sound loose and imagined bringing it up from my feet and up through my torso, chest and throat. I imagined bringing it up through every stupid thing that had gone wrong, through everything that had hurt me or the ones I loved.

I released it into the microphone, and it howled out over the audience. And just like every time before, the intensity of the sound surprised me, as if I didn't even know the full extent of my own voice. The returning roar of the crowd surprised me too. The love they gave was a kind of water that people like me existed on.

The show went by in a daze of sweat and sound and percussion. By the end I was completely wrung out. The crowd had cheered for an encore, and we had given it to them—twice. Eventually, it had been time to leave the stage, and we all did so reluctantly.

Soaking wet and buzzing from adrenaline, we lounged backstage until the early hours and even signed a few autographs for kids who had been given all-access passes. Jake the bodyguard hovered, but even he didn't think the skinny teen girls seeking a signature were a threat, and he allowed himself a much-needed break to grab some food.

The fans were adorable, dressed like me, and they clearly idolized Jamie, Dolly, Jelly and LeeLee. Dolly gave them guitar picks, and Jamie gave them each a busted drumstick, one of which even had some of his blood on it from a wicked rim shot he'd given himself during the encore.

I checked his hands while we all came down from our performance high. His knuckles were beat-up.

"I think there's a first-aid kit in the bathroom," I said, remembering I had seen it earlier. "Let me get you something for your hands."

Jamie grinned. "Always thinking of me," he said.

"No," I said. "I'm just looking out for the band. I wouldn't want to have to replace you," I joked.

He swatted my behind as I walked past. "Hurry back. I have a surprise for you."

"Oh, what is it?" I asked. I loved surprises.

"You'll see."

I hurriedly made my way through a few lingering stagehands to the bathroom and opened the door. I saw the first-aid kit hanging on the wall beside the sink and was just about to open it and look for some bandages and antiseptic when I heard a familiar and menacing voice behind me.

"You're going to need that when I'm through with you, bitch."

I turned slowly to face the voice. It was Mike. He was standing in front of the doorway, blocking the entrance, and he had a knife in his hands.

I suddenly had to pee, and I could hear blood whooshing in my ears. Was it Mike who had made the death threats? Was he there to kill me?

I laughed weakly. "Good one, Mike," I said, pretending I thought he was joking. I hoped he might back off if he figured he wasn't in too deep, but my ploy backfired.

"You think this is funny?" he snarled.

"N-no. Please." I started to cry as I pleaded with him. I didn't want to die.

"That's right, Misery. You beg. Matter of fact, why don't you get on your knees and start begging now."

"Please," I said. "Don't hurt me."

He stepped closer and brandished the knife. "Now, bitch. Kneel."

Slowly I sank to my knees. As he advanced, I saw the bathroom door open a crack. Relief flooded through me as I pictured someone coming to save me. Perhaps it was Jake, back from his food break. My heart fell when I recognized the toe of Jamie's ratty green Converse.

"Hey, what the…?" said Jamie.

Before I could scream, or maybe it was even as I was screaming, I wasn't sure, Mike whirled around and punched at Jamie with the knife.

I jumped up and onto Mike's back, clawing at him and screaming, fighting him with everything I had. He just kept punching at Jamie, who was making horrible wounded sounds.

A few seconds later Jake came through the door like a machine, swiftly taking Mike down, and me with him, then placing Mike in a crushing choke hold that rendered him unconscious.

"Jamie!" I screamed, fighting my way up off the floor.

Jake had already dialed 9-1-1, and his ear was pressed to his cell phone. With his free hand he grabbed my hands and pressed them hard against Jamie's abdomen, where he'd been stabbed.

"Don't let go," Jake said. And, after a brief moment, "I am so sorry I failed you."

I nodded, dazed. This was bad, so very bad, but if it was anyone's fault, it was mine.

I looked down at Jamie. He was trying to reach for something in his pocket. He fumbled and then procured it with trembling fingers. It was a ring box. He tried to hand it to me, but I wouldn't take my hands from his abdomen. I shook my head, unable to speak.

He opened the box. Inside was my mother's ring, the one I had given back to her, the one my dad had passed down to me.

I looked at Jamie, confused. "How?" I whispered. "Why?"

"Kallie," he said, his voice breathless.

I shushed him.

"Keep him talking, Kallie," said Jake. "Keep him awake!"

I saw Jamie's sleepy eyes. The blood loss. Oh god, he was losing a lot of blood.

"What happened?" I asked Jamie. "Where did you get this?"

"I…I got the ring back for you because…" He trailed off.

"But how?" I asked.

"I went to every pawn shop in the city."

"Oh, you silly fool. Why?"

"I couldn't ask your dad for permission," said Jamie. "But I thought I would get it back for you. Do you think he would have given his blessing?"

He got back my ring because he wanted to marry me with it. Of all the foolish, romantic, Jamie-like things to do.

"Yes," I said without hesitation. "Yes, Jamie, he would have given you his permission. In a heartbeat he would have." It was true.

Jamie's eyes began to close.

"Jamie," I cried. "Don't leave me. Baby, please don't leave. Everyone is always leaving me. Please don't go."

"Kallie, when will you learn?"

"What, Jamie? What?"

"At least you had someone to lose…"

He was right. I had him. And Dad. And Jelly and Dolly and LeeLee.

"But I want you, Jamie."

"I know, baby. Kallie, tell me the truth."

"Anything."

"If I had asked you, what would you have said?"

"Yes! Yes, Jamie. I would have said yes a thousand times."

"I wanted the dream," he said sleepily. "I wanted it with you. Is it stupid? Is it stupid I wanted…wanted to put that ugly old ring on your finger, wanted to marry you, get the house for you. I wanted you to have my babies."

He started crying, and I tried to hush him. Every time he sobbed, a fresh gush of bright blood pulsed from his side.

"Jamie, hush. Please. The paramedics are coming. Just hold on, okay?"

"Where is the ambulance?" I hissed at Jake.

"Coming," he said. "Almost here."

"I know it's silly," Jamie continued. "I'm not a real man. I could never be the father of your children."

"Stop it. Stop it right now, Jamie Foster. You are a real man. You are my man. And we could have adopted." I was bawling now. "We still can, Jamie. Please, baby, hold on."

I could see that I was losing him. He was pale and cold and shivering. He had lost so much blood. There was nothing I could do.

"Where is the goddamned ambulance!" I screamed. "Help! Please!"

"Kallie." Jamie was saying my name in a funny, thin little voice.

"I'm here."

"Stay…" he whispered.

"Jamie Foster, if you tell me to 'stay gold,' I swear to God…"

Jamie chuckled a weak, wheezing laugh and then coughed. Blood speckled his cheeks.

"Stay…loud," he said.

He smiled his dazzling Jamie smile, the one that could light me up from inside every single time. And then he was gone.

Chapter Eleven

Mike Michaelson was arrested for murder and was expected to spend the rest of his life in prison.

We had a simple memorial for Jamie. His parents, two people I had barely known and who had seemed like distant shadows in his life, had hugged me hard upon seeing me.

I sang Jamie's song, the one he had written for me, and Dolly accompanied me on guitar. It was hard to sing without bawling, but I made it through, knowing it was important to honor him and the people who loved him.

We're sad without Jamie, but he found a way to send us a message in true Jamie fashion.

Shortly after we came home and unpacked all of our gear, we found a weathered valentine stuffed into the lining of Jamie's bass-drum case. It said:

Kallie,
If you say no, I will still love you.
But please say yes.
No matter what, the band has to stay together.
I love you.
Jamie. xx

I took the valentine/echo and placed it in the tea tin with my dad's echoes. The memories are bittersweet. But at least I had something to lose.

Brooke Carter was born and raised in beautiful British Columbia, where she earned an MFA in Creative Writing (UBC) and currently makes her home with her family. She is the author of a poetry collection, *Poco Loco*, and her work has appeared in numerous literary journals and national magazines. *Another Miserable Love Song* is her first novel.

Titles in the Series

orca soundings

orca soundings

For more information on all the books
in the Orca Soundings series, please visit
www.orcabook.com.